Remembering the Dead

Around the World

Anita Ganeri

heinemann
raintree

Edited by Clare Lewis and Brenda Haugen
Designed by Richard Parker
Picture research by Gina Kammer
Production by Helen McCreath
Originated by Capstone Global Library Ltd
Printed and bound in China by CTPS

19 18 17 16 15
10 9 8 7 6 5 4 3 2 1

Library of Congress Cataloging-in-Publication Data
Ganeri, Anita.
  Remembering the dead around the world / Anita Ganeri.
    pages cm.—(Cultures and customs)
  Includes bibliographical references and index.
  ISBN 978-1-4109-8018-2 (hb)—ISBN 978-1-4109-8023-6 (pb)—ISBN 978-1-4109-8033-5 (ebook) 1. Funeral rites and ceremonies—Juvenile literature. 2. Mourning customs—Juvenile literature. I. Title.
  GT3150.G36 2016
  393'.9—dc23   2015000290

Acknowledgments
We would like to thank the following for permission to reproduce photographs:
Alamy: © Dinodia Photos, 23, © Guillermo Lopez Barrera, 7; AP Photo: Eternal Reefs Inc, 5; Capstone Press (map), throughout; Capstone Studio: Karon Dubke, 28, 29; Corbis: © David Bathgate, 17, © Gideon Mendel, 27, © Robert Wallis, 14, National Geographic Society/© Paul Chesley, 9; Getty Images: ADALBERTO ROQUE, 19, DOUG KANTER, 18, NICOLAS ASFOURI, 8, PHILIPPE LOPEZ, 12, Richard Ellis, 6; Glow Images: Robert Harding/Tim Graham, 22; iStockphoto: EyeJoy, 11, mariusss, 10; National Geographic Creative: IRA BLOCK, 13; Newscom: Eagle Visions P/Craig Lovell, 24, EPA/KIM LUDBROOK, 26, Godong/Philippe Lissac, 15, Mohamed Kadri Xinhua News Agency, 16, REUTERS/ LUC GNAGO, 20, ZUMA Press/Laura Embry, 21, ZUMAPRESS/Subhash Sharma, 25; Shutterstock: Brandon Bourdages, cover

We would like to thank Dr. Suzanne Owen for her invaluable help in the preparation of this book.

Contents

Some words are shown in bold, **like this**. You can find out what they mean by looking in the glossary.

Remembering Loved Ones

In cultures around the world, important events in people's lives are marked with special customs and ceremonies. They help people to celebrate occasions, such as the birth of a baby, a wedding, or remembering a person who has died. They are also a way to guide people from one stage of their lives to the next. This book looks at how people from different cultures and religions mark a person's death.

Around the world, people carry out special ceremonies and **rituals** when a person dies. These include **funerals** and burials, and ways of **mourning** and showing grief. In some cultures, people believe in an afterlife or in **reincarnation** (being born again in a different body). In others, death is truly believed to mark the end of life.

BURIAL AT SEA

A company in the United States offers people the chance to become a "reef ball" when they die. A person's remains are **cremated**, then mixed with concrete to form a ball. The ball is added to an artificial reef that provides a habitat for fish and other sea life.

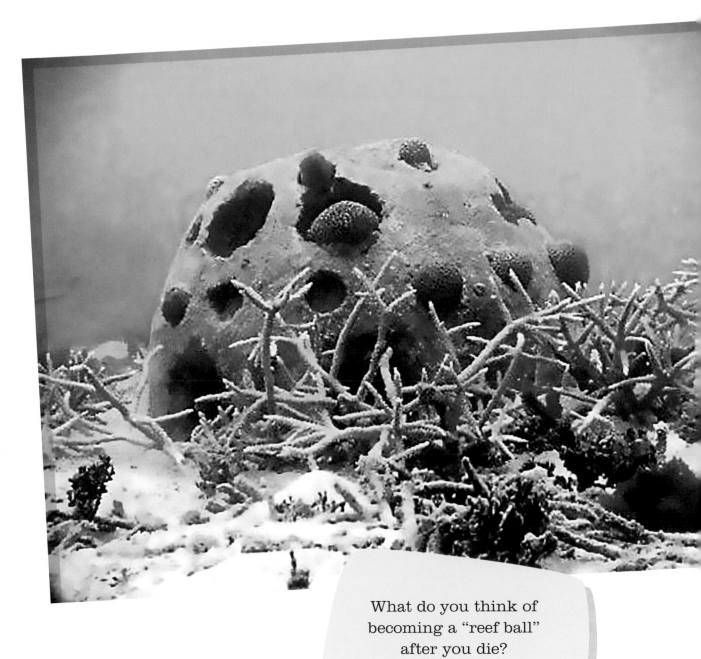

What do you think of becoming a "reef ball" after you die?

Day of the Dead

On November 2, people in Mexico remember people who have died. This is called the Day of the Dead. The celebration dates back hundreds of years to the time of the **Aztecs**.

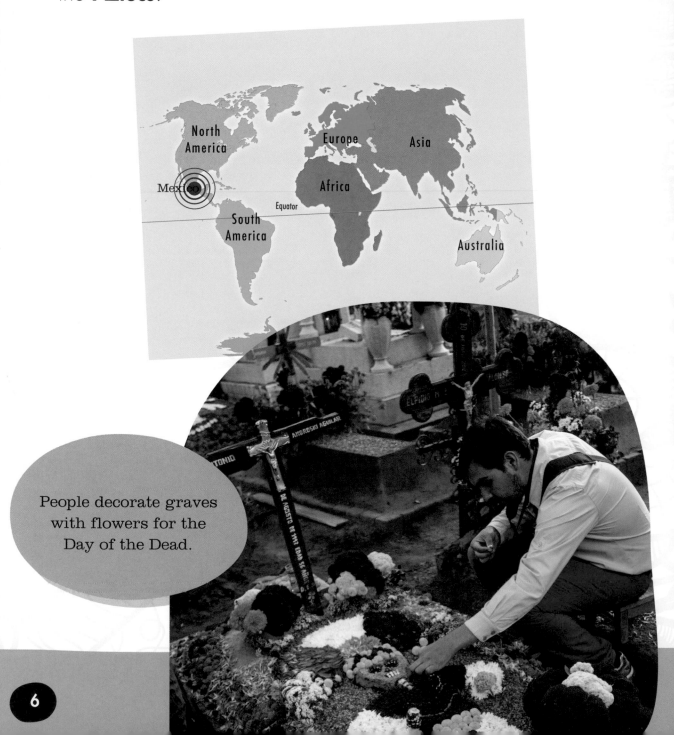

People decorate graves with flowers for the Day of the Dead.

SUGAR SKULLS

For the Day of the Dead, stalls everywhere sell little skulls made from sugar. They are white and decorated in colorful icing, foil, and glitter. People give the skulls as gifts. The name of the person receiving the skull is written on the skull in icing.

Stalls offer sugar skulls for people to give as gifts.

In the days leading up to the Day of the Dead, people visit the graves of their loved ones and decorate them with flowers. They take food and drink, in case their loved ones are hungry or thirsty. They also put out offerings of food on **altars** at home. They leave the windows open at night so that the spirits of their loved ones can come in to eat.

On the day itself, families spend the whole day by the graves, saying prayers for the dead. Some people take a picnic and tell stories about their loved ones. These stories are often funny. The Day of the Dead is supposed to be a happy time.

Smoking Ceremony

Aboriginal people have lived in Australia for thousands of years. When a loved one dies in Aboriginal society, a "smoking ceremony" is held near the dead person's house. People place bunches of green leaves on a small fire to make smoke. The smoke is wafted over the house and mourners. People believe that the smoke will drive away evil spirits. The smoke also cleanses the place and marks a new beginning.

This man is blowing on a bunch of smoldering leaves to make fire for a smoking ceremony.

After the ceremony, there is a big feast with singing and dancing. The mourners paint themselves with red ocher (clay), again to scare away evil. Traditionally, in northern parts of Australia, the dead person's body is placed on top of a wooden platform outside the village and covered in leaves. Then it is left to rot away.

CEREMONY FOR A BABY

Smoking ceremonies are also held at other important times, such as the birth of a baby. Aboriginal people believe that the smoke will help the baby to grow up to be strong and healthy. If a child is sick, another smoking ceremony is held to help it get better.

Jewish Funeral

A **Jewish funeral** takes place as soon as possible after a person has died. This is usually within 24 hours. According to tradition, most Jews are buried, although today some are **cremated** instead.

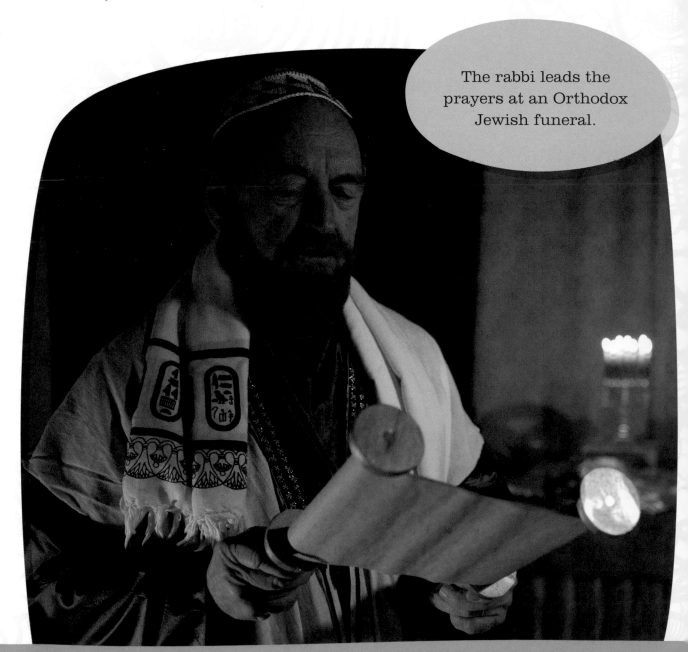

The rabbi leads the prayers at an Orthodox Jewish funeral.

The Yahrzeit candle is lit on the anniversary of the person's death.

The funeral service is very simple, with a plain **coffin** and no flowers. This shows that everyone, rich or poor, is equal before God. At the **cemetery**, a **rabbi** leads the prayers and reads from the **Torah**, the Jewish holy book. He also talks about the life and achievements of the person who has died.

LIGHTING A CANDLE

Each year, on the anniversary of his or her death, the dead person's name is read out in the **synagogue**. At home, relatives light a special candle, called a Yahrzeit (say "yart-site"), which burns for 24 hours. They also recite the Kaddish, which is the Jewish prayer for the dead.

For seven days after a death, the family stays at home to mourn their loved one. This is called "sitting Shivah" (*Shivah* means "seven"). Every evening, friends and relatives visit the house to offer prayers and sympathy to the family.

Funeral Gifts

There are many rules around death in Chinese culture. People believe that bad luck will come to the family if it does not follow the rules properly.

At a **funeral** in China, family and friends bring **wreaths** of white flowers, such as irises. White is the traditional color of **mourning** in Chinese culture. The flowers are placed around the body, which is laid in an open **coffin**. People also bring white envelopes, filled with money. This is given to the family to help pay for the funeral.

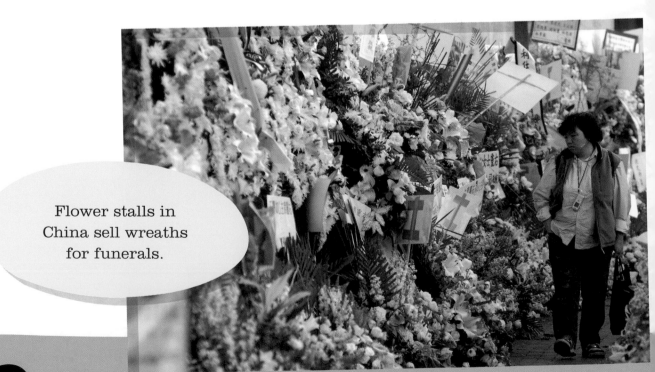

Flower stalls in China sell wreaths for funerals.

Professional mourners join the procession at a Chinese funeral.

PAID TO MOURN

At some Chinese funerals, the family hires **professional** mourners to make sure that their loved one is given a good, lively send-off. The mourners are paid to cry, wail, and sing sad songs and are often accompanied by a band.

In return, the family gives each guest a white or red envelope with a coin, a piece of candy, a handkerchief, and a piece of red thread inside. The coin is to make sure that the guest returns home safely. Guests take the red thread home and tie it to the front door of their house to keep evil spirits away.

Colors of mourning

In different cultures, different colors are linked to death. In some countries, people wear black clothes to **funerals**. The black color matches the sadness of the occasion. In Europe, this tradition dates back to Roman times, when men wore dark-colored **togas** during times of **mourning**. In some countries, such as Spain, **widows** may wear black clothes for the rest of their lives.

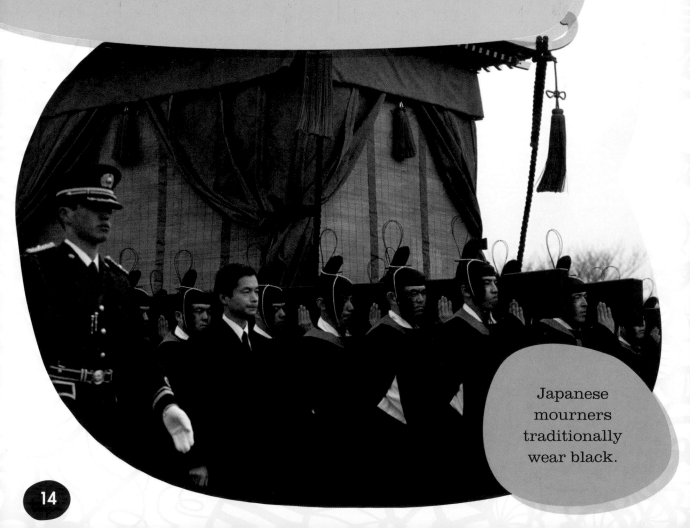

Japanese mourners traditionally wear black.

Chinese colors

In Chinese culture, only the dead person's closest relatives wear black. Any grandchildren, aunts, uncles, and cousins wear blue. Other mourners, who are not as close to the dead person, wear white and other bright colors. People do not wear red clothes, because red is the color of happiness.

Widows in white

In the **Hindu** religion, white is the color of mourning. A Hindu widow wears a plain white **sari**, with very little jewelry. She also removes the red mark that she has worn on her forehead since she was married.

From the time of her husband's death, a Hindu widow dresses in white.

Mourning rings

For hundreds of years in the United Kingdom, it was the custom for people to wear mourning rings to remember loved ones who had died. The rings were often made from gold and black **jet** and, often, a lock of the dead person's hair.

Watched by Angels

If possible, a **Muslim funeral** should take place on the same day that a person dies. The body is washed and wrapped in white cloth. It is taken in a **coffin** to the **mosque**, where the **imam** recites the funeral prayers. After this, the coffin is taken to the **cemetery**.

Muslims are buried facing toward the holy city of Mecca. During their lives, this is the direction they face when they pray every day. The grave is marked with a simple stone.

Mourners at a Muslim funeral carry the coffin to the cemetery.

Muslims are sad to lose a loved one but are comforted in their faith. They believe that every person is watched by two angels, who keep a record of the person's good and bad deeds. This record is handed to **Allah** on the Day of Judgment. People who have lived good lives, according to Allah's wishes, will go to Paradise. Wicked people will go to Hell.

DYING WORDS

The **Prophet Muhammad** said that the last words a dying Muslim should hear are those of the Shahadah. This is a special prayer that expresses what Muslims believe.

"There is no God but Allah.

And Muhammad is his messenger."

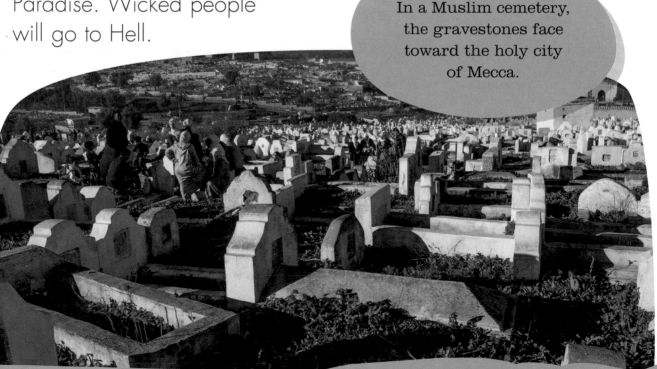

In a Muslim cemetery, the gravestones face toward the holy city of Mecca.

Jazz Funeral

In the city of New Orleans, Louisiana, some people from African American communities, mostly musicians, have a **jazz funeral**. A funeral begins with a service in a Christian church. Then a jazz band plays sad, marching music as the **coffin** is taken to the **cemetery**. After leaving the cemetery, the music changes and the band strikes up much livelier, happier tunes. Everyone sings and dances along to celebrate the life of the person who has died.

This jazz band is playing at a jazz funeral in New Orleans.

The roots of the jazz funeral date back to Africa. Music is an important part of funerals in many African countries. The Yoruba people of Nigeria dance, sing, and play drums. They believe that this helps to keep the dead person's spirit happy. The **ancestors** of many African Americans came to the United States as slaves and brought their customs with them.

FUNERAL MUSIC

Around the world, music is often played at funerals. This may be a religious song, such as a hymn, or a piece of music that had a special connection to the dead person. In one poll of the most popular funeral songs, "My Way" by Frank Sinatra topped the list.

A Yoruba funeral is marked with dancing, singing, and drumming.

Around the World

After a person dies, his or her body may be placed in a **coffin**, ready to be buried or **cremated**. Coffins come in many sizes and shapes.

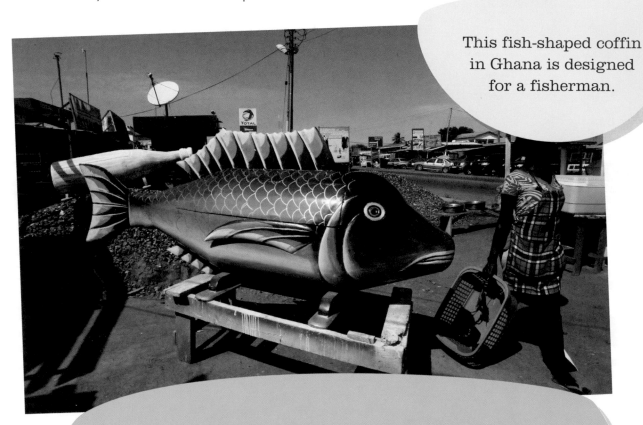

This fish-shaped coffin in Ghana is designed for a fisherman.

Amazing coffins

In Ghana, some people are buried in brightly colored coffins that represent their life or work. Examples include fish- or boat-shaped coffins for fishermen; Bible-shaped coffins for churchgoers; piano-shaped coffins for musicians; and even camera-shaped coffins for photographers.

Eco-coffins

In some Western countries, people choose to be buried or cremated in coffins that do not harm the environment. This means using coffins made from materials that rot away quickly and easily, such as bamboo, willow, and even cloth and cardboard.

Another unusual eco-coffin is shaped like an egg and made from **bioplastic**. The body is placed inside and the egg is planted in the ground, like a bulb. A tree is planted on top.

These people are decorating a cardboard eco-coffin with scenes from nature.

Tree burials

The Caviteno people of the Philippines do not use coffins for their dead. Instead, they bury them standing upright inside a hollowed-out tree trunk. The dying person chooses the tree when he or she gets sick or grows very old.

Many
Lives

Hindus do not believe that death is the end of life. They believe in **reincarnation**, where a person's soul lives on after death and is born again in a new body—human or animal. People's next life depends on how they lived their current life. If they have acted well, they will be reborn in a better life. If they have acted badly, their next life will be a worse one.

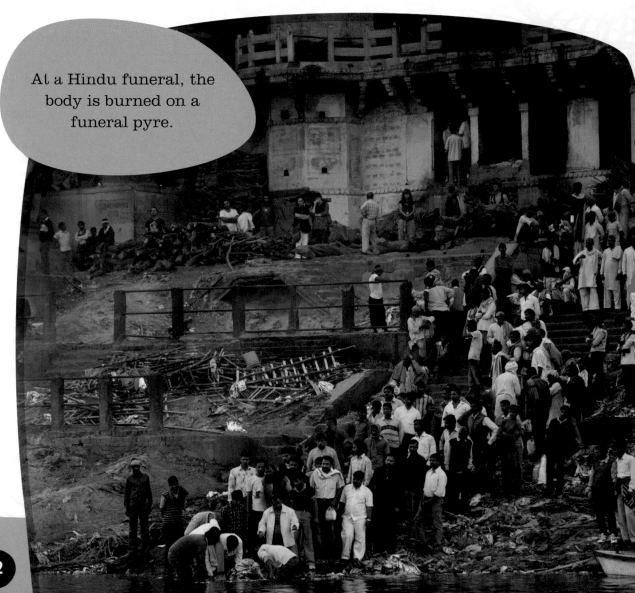

At a Hindu funeral, the body is burned on a funeral pyre.

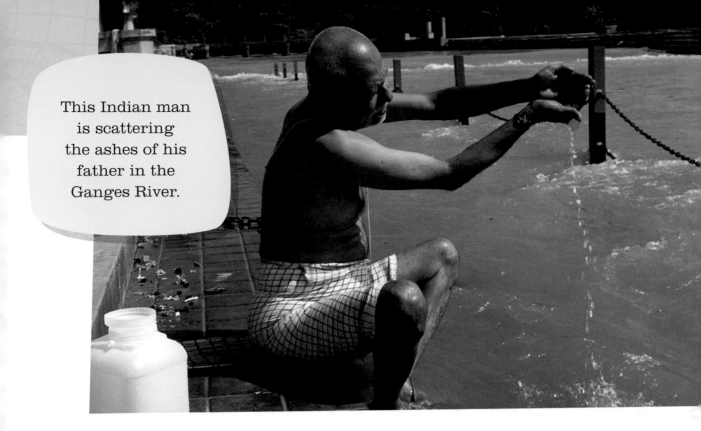

This Indian man is scattering the ashes of his father in the Ganges River.

Funeral pyre

At a Hindu **funeral**, the body is always **cremated**. Traditionally in India, the body is placed on a large platform of logs and sandalwood, called a **pyre**. The eldest son, or a close male relative, walks around the pyre seven times. Then he lights the fire while a priest chants verses from the Hindu sacred books.

SACRED RIVER

Three days after the funeral, the relatives collect the ashes. If possible, they scatter them in the Ganges River. It is a sacred river for Hindus. They believe that the water of the Ganges washes away people's sins.

After the funeral, there are 10 or 12 days of **mourning**. On the last day, Hindus believe that the person's soul has found a new body.

Sky Burials

In much of Tibet, the ground is too rocky or hard to dig a grave and there is not much firewood for building **funeral pyres**. A dead body is carried to a mountainside and left for the vultures to eat. Most Tibetans are **Buddhists**. They believe that this is a good and generous way to dispose of a body because it provides food for other living things.

BIRDS AND ANGELS

Like **Hindus**, Buddhists believe that a dead person's soul is born again in a new body. Tibetans believe that the vultures are like angels. They carry the dead person's soul up into the heavens, where it waits to be reborn.

These vultures gather around a sky burial site in Tibet.

Towers of silence

According to **Zoroastrian** beliefs, a dead body is unclean. It must not be allowed to touch earth, fire, or water. To avoid this, a dead person's body is placed on top of a tall stone tower for the vultures to eat. The tower is called a dakhma, or tower of silence. Some time later, the bones are collected in a pit in the center of the tower. Over a long time, they gradually wear away.

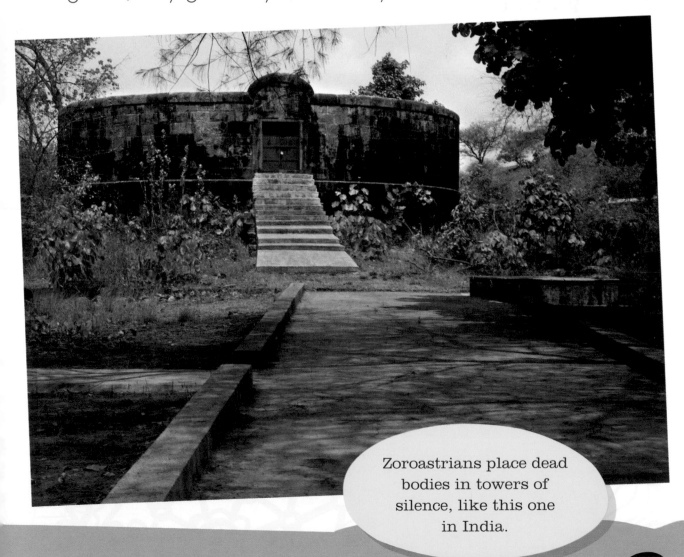

Zoroastrians place dead bodies in towers of silence, like this one in India.

Turning the Bones

The people of Madagascar have an unusual ceremony for remembering their dead. It is called famadihana, which means "the turning of the bones." Every five or seven years, a family visits its family tomb, where the bones of their dead relatives lie, wrapped in cloth. The bones are taken out and sprayed with perfume. Then, as a band plays, members of the family take turns dancing with the bones.

People carry the wrapped bones of their ancestors at famadihana.

Families dance together as they carry the bones in white cloths.

This ceremony may sound gruesome, but in Malagasy culture, it is a way of thanking and showing respect to those who have died. People tell stories about their relatives and ask for their blessing. It is also a chance for a family reunion—relatives come from across the country to take part in the celebrations.

RESPECT FOR ANCESTORS

In Malagasy culture, people show great respect to their razana (**ancestors**). They believe that the ancestors have the power to affect the lives and fortunes of the living, and that there will be great hardship or trouble if they are offended.

Afterward, the bones are wrapped in fresh cloth and placed back in the tomb.

Decorate a **Day** of the **Dead Skull**

Mexicans celebrate the Day of the Dead by making beautiful sugar skulls (see page 7). They are decorated to look friendly and colorful and are given as gifts. Make your own skull decorations using scrap paper.

- two sheets of scrap paper
- a large bowl
- flour
- water
- white glue
- a strainer
- parchment paper
- paints and other decorations
- scissors
- paintbrush

1 Tear the paper into small squares and put them into a bowl. Add a tablespoon of flour.

2 Ask an adult to help you add hot water from the faucet. Leave the paper and flour to soak for three hours.

3 Rub and squish the paper with your fingers to make a pulp. Put the mixture into a strainer and squeeze out as much water as possible.

4 Put the pulp back into the bowl. Add a tablespoon of glue and knead with your hands until the mixture feels like clay.

28

5 Trace the outline of a skull on a piece of parchment paper. Build up a skull shape using small balls of the paper pulp.

6 Use the bottom of a pencil to make dents for eyes, and the pointed tip of the pencil to mark the nose and teeth.

7 Leave the paper skull to dry for two to three days. Then add a coat of white paint.

9 Trim the paper at the edges. Brush on a coat of watered-down glue to seal your design.

8 Decorate your skull using bright colors and shapes such as flowers, dots, and swirls. Mexicans often add beads, sequins, and glitter, too.

Remember, these skulls are just for decoration and NOT for eating!

Glossary

Allah Islamic name for God, in the Arabic language

altar place where offerings such as food and flowers are made to gods and ancestors

ancestor relative from the past

Aztecs people who lived in Mexico hundreds of years ago

bioplastic type of plastic made from plant oil that breaks down more quickly than ordinary plastic

Buddhist person who follows the religion of Buddhism

cemetery place where dead people are buried

coffin box in which a dead person's body is buried or cremated

cremated when a dead person's body is burned

funeral ceremony at which a dead person's body is buried or cremated

Hindu person who follows the Hindu religion

imam religious leader

jazz lively type of music

jet hard, black stone

Jewish connected with the religion of Judaism. A Jew is a person who follows Judaism.

mosque place of worship

mourning feeling and showing sadness that a person has died

Muslim person who follows the religion of Islam

professional person who is paid for what he or she does as a job

Prophet Muhammad last and greatest in a line of messengers sent by Allah to teach people how to live in the Muslim religion

pyre pile of wood on which a dead body is placed for cremation

rabbi Jewish religious teacher

reincarnation belief that a person is born again after he or she dies

ritual ceremony with set ways of doing things

sari traditional dress worn by many women in India

synagogue Jewish place of worship

toga robe worn by some men in Roman times

Torah part of the Jewish holy book

widow wife whose husband has died

wreath ring of flowers, sometimes placed on a person's grave

Zoroastrian person who follows the religion of Zoroastrianism

Find Out More

Books

Jones, Aled. *What Do You Believe?: Religion and Faith in the World Today*. New York: Dorling Kindersley, 2011.

Meredith, Susan. *The Usbourne Encyclopedia of World Religions* (Internet-Linked Encyclopedias). Tulsa, OK.: EDC, 2010.

Rohr, Ian. *Religious Celebrations* (Celebrations). Mankato, MN.: Smart Apple Media, 2011.

Web sites

Facthound offers a safe, fun way to find Internet sites related to this book. All of the sites on Facthound have been researched by our staff.

Here's all you do:

Visit www.facthound.com

Type in this code: 9781410980182

Further research

It is sad when someone dies, but it is also a time for remembering the happy times that you shared with that person. Some people write poems or stories to help them remember loved ones. Can you find some of these in books or on the Internet?

Index